Elements of Reading

Level A

Vocabulary

Isabel L. Beck, Ph.D., and Margaret G. McKeown, Ph.D.

D1469556

This book belongs to

_____

- -

_____

Harcourt Achieve
Rigby · Steck-Vaughn

www.HarcourtAchieve.com
1.800.531.5015

Acknowledgments

Editorial Director Stephanie Muller

Lead Editor Terra Tarango

Design Team Cynthia Ellis, Cynthia Hannon, Joan Cunningham

Production Team Mychael Ferris-Pacheco, Paula Schumann, Alan Klemp

Editorial, Design, and Production Development The Quarasan Group, Inc.

Illustrations: Angela Adams 20-21, 44-45; Elizabeth Allen 8-9, 52-53, 76-77; Marla Baggetta 43; Cathy Beylon 19; Elizabeth Buttler 47, 79; Donna Catanese 18; Roberta Collier-Morales 58, 87; Carolyn Croll 14; Renee Daily 70; Sally Davies 24-25; Nancy Didion iii; Len Ebert 72-73; Rusty Fletcher 30, 94; Kersti Frigell 31, 66; Diane Greenseid 7, 34; Amanda Harvey 32-33, 64-65, 96-97; Meryl Henderson 56-57, 86; Richard Hoit 55; Benrei Huang 78; Nicole in den Bosch 74; Lauren Klementz-Harte 36-37, 68-69; Thea Kliros 82; Susan Lexa 88-89; Kathryn Mitter 3, 50, 75; Suzanne Mogensen 67; Ana Ochoa 28-29; Ed Olson 90; Kathleen O'Malley 16-17; Laura Ovresat 12-13; Judith Pfeiffer 4-5, 80-81; Marcy Ramsey 60-61, 92-93; Nicole Rutten 15; Miriam Sagasti 6; Reg Sandland 2, 35; Patricia Schoonover 42; Sally Springer 23; Bridget Starr-Taylor 4; Lydia Taranovic 48-49, 84-85; Joan Waites 11, 46; Laura Watson 1; Teri Weidner 26, 51; Bari Weissman 22; Marsha Winborn 40-41; Jason Wolff 95

ISBN 0-7398-8446-8

© 2005 Harcourt Achieve Inc.

Printed in China   2   3   4   5   6   7   8   9   10   985   08   07   06   05   04

Dear Teacher,

This Student Book is full of lively, fun-filled activities that provide ample opportunities for children to practice using new words.

The vocabulary words in this book are meant to increase children's oral vocabulary skills, so the activities are designed to be led by the teacher. Use the teacher notes at the bottom of each page in conjunction with the Word Chats in the Teacher's Guide to facilitate engaging discussions surrounding these activities.

While this book is for children, we hope that you will have fun, too! The more you use and have fun with new words, the more children will enjoy and use them, too.

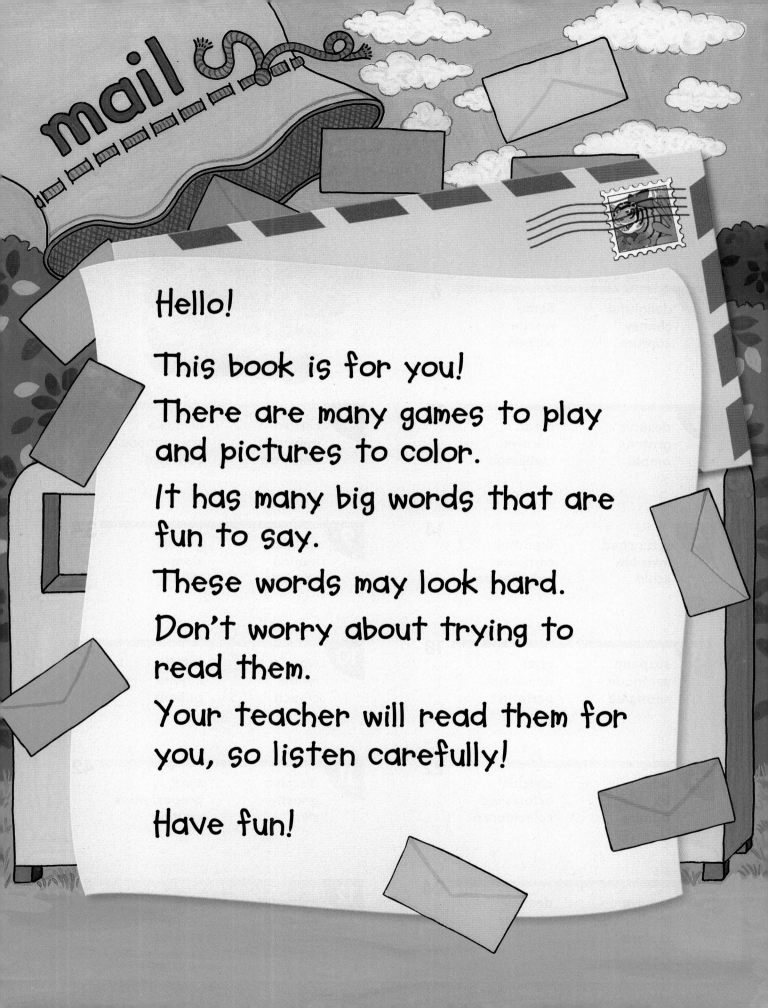

Hello!

This book is for you!

There are many games to play and pictures to color.

It has many big words that are fun to say.

These words may look hard.

Don't worry about trying to read them.

Your teacher will read them for you, so listen carefully!

Have fun!

Contents

1 Circle the person who is **versatile**.

2 Draw a line under the pet that is **lively**.

3 Draw a box around something that **glimmers**.

Teacher: Read aloud each numbered item as children complete the activity. Ask children to explain how they chose each item in the picture.

Listen. Draw.

1 Draw a line from the word to each thing that can be **comforting**.

bed

car

comforting

teddy bear

brick

2 Draw a line from the word to each thing that has an **expression**.

doll

clock

expression

boy

dog

3 Draw a line from the word to each thing that is **fleet**.

snail

fleet

rabbit

horse

turtle

Teacher: Read aloud each numbered item. Have children draw a line to the pictures that best show each word. Let them know that there may be more than one picture for each word. Ask them why they chose the pictures they did.

1 Which picture shows an animal that is **lively**?

○   ○   ○

2 Which picture shows a person who is **fleet**?

○   ○   ○

3 Which picture shows something that is **comforting**?

○   ○   ○

Teacher: Read aloud each numbered item and have children fill in the bubble under the best picture.

4 Which picture shows something that **glimmers**?

○   ○   ○

5 Which picture shows a boy with a surprised **expression**?

○   ○   ○

6 Which picture shows someone who is **versatile**?

○   ○   ○

Listen. Read. Color.

1 **capture** — Color purple.

3 **fierce** — Color green.

2 **rescue** — Color red.

grab

help

catch

save

mean

Teacher: Read aloud each vocabulary word and its assigned color. Have children use that color for each part of the picture with a word that has to do with that vocabulary word. Continue with the remaining words until the hidden picture is revealed. Ask children how each word they colored is related to the vocabulary word.

Listen. Draw.

1 Circle the people who are in **suspense**.

2 Draw a line under the pet that is **clumsy**.

3 Draw a box around the people who are having a **delightful** time.

Teacher: Read aloud each numbered item as children complete the activity. Ask children to explain how they chose each item in the picture.

1 Which picture shows a **clumsy** dog?

○   ○   ○

2 Which picture shows a **delightful** time?

○   ○   ○

3 Which picture shows a boy in **suspense**?

○   ○   ○

Teacher: Read aloud each numbered item and have children fill in the bubble under the best picture.

4 Which picture shows a woman **rescuing** someone?

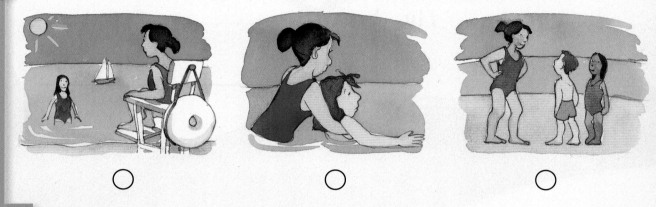

○   ○   ○

5 Which picture shows birds that have been **captured**?

○   ○   ○

6 Which picture shows a **fierce** animal?

○   ○   ○

1 Write the word that is like the word **amble**.

walk fly

hop run

_____
- - - - - - - - - - - - - -
_____

2 Write the word that is like the word **plead**.

_____
- - - - - - - - - - - - - -
_____

clap

beg

fall

stop

3 Write the word that has to do with the word **challenge**.

milk
cat

day
try

_____
- - - - - - - - - - - - - -
_____

Teacher: Read aloud each numbered item. Have children read the answer choices independently and write the best answer for each item. Then have children explain their choices.

Listen. Circle.

1

deserve   plead

2

deceive   amble

3

amble   grateful

4

deceive   challenge

Teacher: Read aloud the two vocabulary words for each picture. Ask children to circle the word that best goes with each picture. Ask children how the word they chose goes with the picture.

1 Which picture shows a **grateful** boy?

○ ○ ○

2 Which picture shows a girl who **deserves** a rest?

○ ○ ○

3 Which picture shows a girl who might be **challenging** someone?

○ ○ ○

Teacher: Read aloud each numbered item and have children fill in the bubble under the best picture.

4 Which picture shows a boy **deceiving** his mom?

○ ○ ○

5 Which picture shows a girl **pleading**?

○ ○ ○

6 Which picture shows a girl **ambling**?

○ ○ ○

1 Draw a line from the word to each thing that is being **scrunched**.

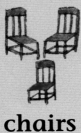

chairs

paper

cups

scrunched

clothes

2 Draw a line from the word to each thing that is **dreadful**.

weather

noise

dreadful

flowers

worm

3 Draw a line from the word to each thing that looks like it is **exaggerated**.

jump

exaggerate

lift

climb

fly

Teacher: Read aloud each numbered item. Have children draw a line to the pictures that best show each word. Let them know that there may be more than one picture for each word. Ask them why they chose the pictures they did.

14

Listen. Draw.

1 Circle the dog that is trying to be **invisible**.

2 Draw a line under the dog that is being **scolded**.

3 Draw a box around the boy who is **complaining**.

Teacher: Read aloud each numbered item as children complete the activity. Ask children to explain how they chose each item in the picture.

15

Show What You Know

Listen. Fill in the bubble.

1 Which picture shows an **invisible** bike?

○　　　　　　　○　　　　　　　○

2 Which picture shows a boy **complaining**?

○　　　　　　　○　　　　　　　○

3 Which picture shows something **dreadful**?

○　　　　　　　○　　　　　　　○

Teacher: Read aloud each numbered item and have children fill in the bubble under the best picture.

4 Which picture shows people **scrunched** in a car?

○   ○   ○

5 Which picture shows a girl being **scolded**?

○   ○   ○

6 A boy would be **exaggerating** if he said he could do which of these things?

○   ○   ○

1 The class did something nice.
They gave Mr. Brown
a **serenade**.

2 Mark put together
a model plane.
His dad helped
him **suspend** it.

3 Amber passed food
to a woman in
a **ridiculous** hat.

18

Teacher: Read aloud each numbered item as children read along silently. Then have children circle the best
picture for each numbered item. Ask children why they chose each picture they did.

Listen. Circle.

1

suspend   spangled

2

perform   serenade

3

pride   ridiculous

4

suspend   ridiculous

Teacher: Read aloud the two vocabulary words for each picture. Ask children to circle the word that best goes with each picture. Ask children how the word they chose goes with the picture.

19

Show What You Know

Listen. Fill in the bubble.

1 Which picture shows a dog **performing**?

○   ○   ○

2 Which picture shows something **suspended**?

○   ○   ○

3 Which person feels **pride**?

○   ○   ○

Teacher: Read aloud each numbered item and have children fill in the bubble under the best picture.

4 ▸ Which picture is **ridiculous**?

  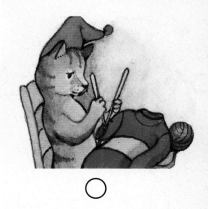

○　　　　　　　　○　　　　　　　　○

5 ▸ Which object is **spangled**?

 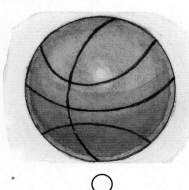 

○　　　　　　　　○　　　　　　　　○

6 ▸ Which girl is listening to a **serenade**?

○　　　　　　　　○　　　　　　　　○

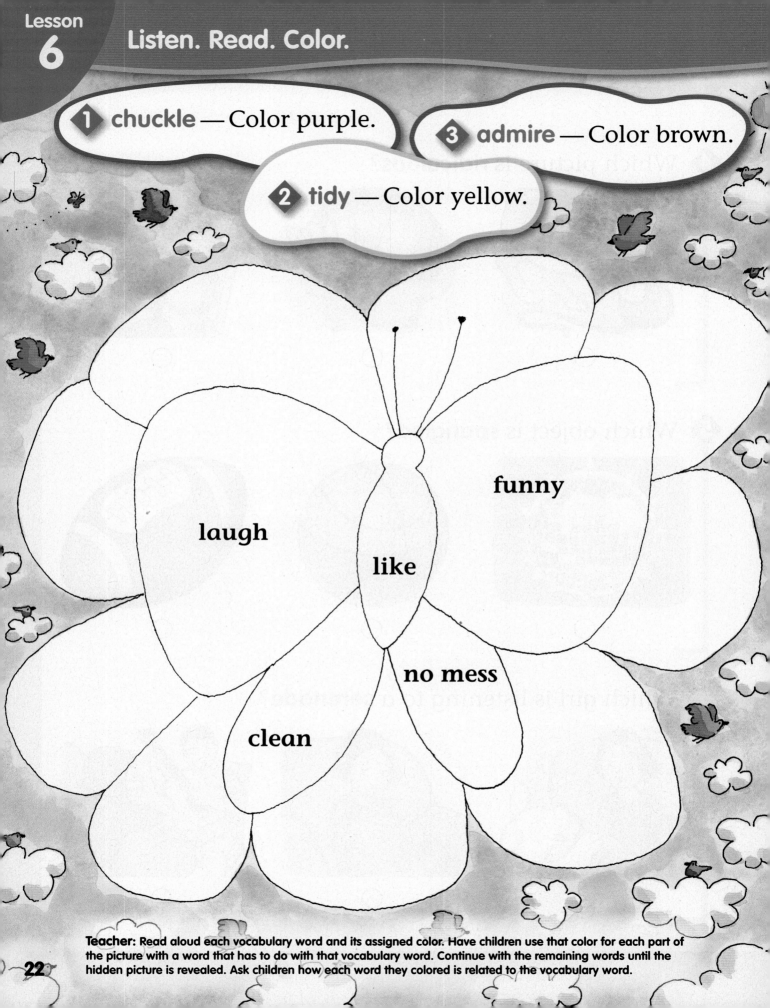

1 chuckle — Color purple.

2 tidy — Color yellow.

3 admire — Color brown.

funny

laugh

like

no mess

clean

Teacher: Read aloud each vocabulary word and its assigned color. Have children use that color for each part of the picture with a word that has to do with that vocabulary word. Continue with the remaining words until the hidden picture is revealed. Ask children how each word they colored is related to the vocabulary word.

Listen. Draw.

1 Draw a box around the person who is **astonished**.

2 Draw a line under the **coincidence**.

3 Circle the girl who is **irking** someone.

Teacher: Read aloud each numbered item as children complete the activity. Ask children to explain how they chose each item in the picture.

23

1 Which picture shows a **coincidence**?

○ ○ ○

2 Which picture shows a dog **irking** its owner?

○ ○ ○

3 Which picture shows a man who is **astonished**?

○ ○ ○

Teacher: Read aloud each numbered item and have children fill in the bubble under the best picture.

4 Which picture shows a room that is **tidy**?

○ ○ ○

5 Which picture shows a girl **chuckling**?

○ ○ ○

6 Which picture shows a boy **admiring** something?

  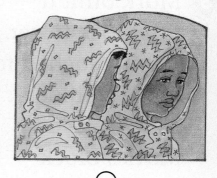

○ ○ ○

1 Beth does something for her dog every day. Today she is giving her dog something it needs to **survive**.

2 It was snowing in the woods. The rabbits found **shelter** until it stopped snowing.

3 Mark built a tall block tower. Frank reached for a pile of blocks. He **destroyed** Mark's block tower.

Teacher: Read aloud each numbered item as children read along silently. Then have children circle the best picture for each numbered item. Ask children why they chose each picture they did.

1 Write the word that is like the word **disturb**.

bed

feed

upset

help

_____

- -

_____

2 Write the word that is like the word **dwell**.

_____

- -

_____

live

sing

zip

mix

3 Write the word that is like the word **observe**.

watch

send

wet

save

_____

- -

_____

Teacher: Read aloud each numbered item. Have children read the answer choices independently and write the best answer for each item. Then have children explain their choices.

27

1 Which of these do you use to **observe**?

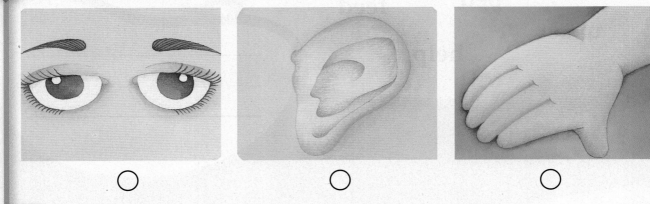

○   ○   ○

2 Which picture shows a beaver who is **sheltered**?

○   ○   ○

3 Which picture shows a kite that is **destroyed**?

○   ○   ○

Teacher: Read aloud each numbered item and have children fill in the bubble under the best picture.

4 Which picture shows a girl **disturbing** a cat?

○ ○ ○

5 Which do you need to **survive**?

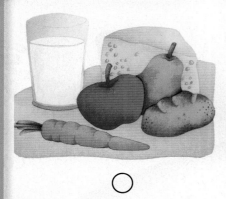  

○ ○ ○

6 Which shows a place to **dwell**?

○ ○ ○

1 Draw a line from the word to each thing that can be a **disguise**.

mask

wig

shoes

disguise

glasses

shirt

2 Draw a line from the word to each thing that might be **scrumptious**.

apple

turkey

cap

scrumptious

toy

cake

3 Draw a line from the word to each thing that can **quiver**.

feather

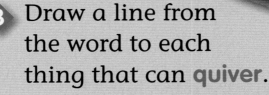
quiver

jelly

house

rock

arrow

Teacher: Read aloud each numbered item. Have children draw a line to the pictures that best show each word. Let them know that there may be more than one picture for each word. Ask them why they chose the pictures they did.

Listen. Draw.

1 Draw a box around the girl who is **certain** she will get a hot dog.

2 Circle the boy who is trying to **convince** his mom.

3 Draw a line under the dog that **outsmarted** the man.

Teacher: Read aloud each numbered item as children complete the activity. Ask children to explain how they chose each item in the picture.

1 Which picture shows something **quivering**?

○   ○   ○

2 Which picture shows a girl wearing a **disguise**?

○   ○   ○

3 Which picture shows a girl **outsmarting** her friend?

○   ○   ○

Teacher: Read aloud each numbered item and have children fill in the bubble under the best picture.

4 Which picture shows a boy who is **certain** he knows the answer?

     ◯   ◯   ◯

5 Which picture shows a boy trying to **convince** his friend to play?

     ◯   ◯   ◯

6 Which picture shows something that might be **scrumptious**?

     ◯   ◯   ◯

1

squiggle

sloppy

mound

Joe wanted to help out in the yard.

He began to rake the leaves.

He raked all morning.

By noon, the yard was clean.

All the leaves had been
raked into a big, round pile.

sprinkle

gobble

tribute

2

Ann and Mary love the chicken soup
that Mom cooks.

This morning they smelled
the soup when they woke up.

They waited and waited for
the soup to be ready.

Finally, they heard Mom
say, "Come and eat!"

Ann and Mary ran to the table.

They ate all the soup up right away!

Teacher: For each story, read aloud the vocabulary words and then have children read the story independently.
Have children circle the vocabulary word that best describes the story. Ask children why the word they chose was
the best one for each story.

34

Listen. Circle.

1

mound   tribute

2

sloppy   sprinkle

3

squiggle   gobble

4

tribute   sloppy

Teacher: Read aloud the two vocabulary words for each picture. Ask children to circle the word that best goes with each picture. Ask children how the word they chose goes with the picture.

35

1 Which picture shows a **sloppy** boy?

○ ○ ○

2 Which picture shows a **tribute**?

○ ○ ○

3 Which picture shows a girl **sprinkling** something on a cake?

○ ○ ○

Teacher: Read aloud each numbered item and have children fill in the bubble under the best picture.

4 Which picture shows a **mound**?

  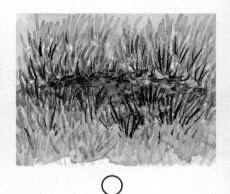

○ ○ ○

5 Which picture shows **squiggles**?

○ ○ ○

6 Which picture shows a man who is **gobbling** his food?

○ ○ ○

1 Write the word that has to do with the word **wander**.

walk

jump

run

spin

_____

- - - - - - - - - - - - - - - - - -

_____

2 Write the word that is like the word **inquire**.

_____

- - - - - - - - - - - - - - - - - -

_____

ask

yell

nap

look

3 Write the word of the thing **artistic** people do better than other people.

sleep

laugh

draw

eat

_____

- - - - - - - - - - - - - - - - - -

_____

Teacher: Read aloud each numbered item. Have children read the answer choices independently and write the best answer for each item. Then have children explain their choices.

Listen. Read. Write.

1 My rabbit Pinky likes to **nibble** on carrots.

_____

- -

She takes _____ bites

of them.

tiny

huge

ten

2 Liza had to **crouch** to see under her bed.

_____

- -

She had to _____

her knees.

kick

bend

rub

3 Michael is very **artistic**.

_____

- -

He is _____ at drawing.

bad

funny

good

4 Juan was **patient** in the long line.

_____

- -

He stayed _____

while he waited for his turn.

angry

sad

calm

Teacher: Read aloud each numbered item. Then have children read the answer choices and write the best answer to complete each sentence. Have children explain why they wrote the words they did.

39

1 Which picture shows a girl being **artistic**?

○   ○   ○

2 Which picture shows a boy who is being **patient**?

○   ○   ○

3 Which picture shows an animal that would **nibble** its food?

○   ○   ○

Teacher: Read aloud each numbered item and have children fill in the bubble under the best picture.

4 Which picture shows a monkey **crouching**?

○   ○   ○

5 Which picture shows someone who is **wandering**?

○   ○   ○

6 Which picture shows a boy who wants to **inquire** about something?

○   ○   ○

1 swift—Color yellow.

3 ghastly—Color brown.

2 sly—Color pink.

4 preposterous—Color red.

not true

run

fast

race

hurry

tricky

foxy

clever

terrible

scary

Teacher: Read aloud each vocabulary word and its assigned color. Have children use that color for each part of the picture with a word that has to do with that vocabulary word. Continue with the remaining words until the hidden picture is revealed. Ask children how each word they colored is related to the vocabulary word.

Listen. Read. Circle.

1

Mike was riding his new bike.

There was a big hole in the sidewalk.

Mike did not know about the hole.

Lisa shouted, "Look out!"

Mike quickly stopped.

He thanked Lisa for the warning.

preposterous

caution

sly

swift

ghastly

dissolved

2

Cathy's uncle does something fun.

He makes statues out of ice.

He made a beautiful one for Cathy.

The next day, her friend came to see it.

Oh no! It melted! It was gone!

Teacher: For each story, read aloud the vocabulary words and then have children read the story independently. Have children circle the vocabulary word that best describes the story. Ask children why the word they chose was the best one for each story.

1 Which picture shows something **preposterous**?

○   ○   ○

2 Which picture shows a ball moving **swiftly**?

○   ○   ○

3 Which picture shows someone being **sly**?

○   ○   ○

Teacher: Read aloud each numbered item and have children fill in the bubble under the best picture.

4 Which picture shows a **ghastly** mask?

○   ○   ○

5 Which picture shows something **dissolving**?

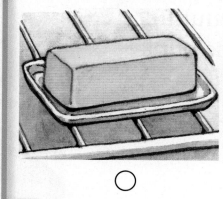      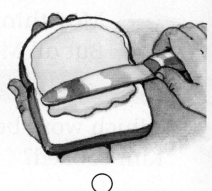

○   ○   ○

6 Which picture shows someone **cautioning** someone else?

○   ○   ○

Dinner for May

Kim is cooking dinner for her sister May.
She cooks turkey and peas and pie.
She cooks more food than May could
ever eat.

Kim wants the dinner table to look
just right.
She moves the forks from here to there.
She changes where she puts the plates.

May says the food smells tasty.
May thinks the table looks beautiful.
But all May eats is a thin piece of pie!

1 Which word best tells about how much food
Kim cooked?

> sliver   amazed   surplus

2 Which word best tells about what Kim did with
the forks and plates?

> rearrange   tremendous   palate

3 Which word best tells how much pie May ate?

> tremendous   surplus   sliver

Teacher: Have children read the story independently. Ask a volunteer to read each question aloud. Then read the word choices to children and have them circle the best answer. Ask children why they chose the words they did.

tremendous

amazed

palate

giant

taste

shocked

large

huge

surprised

Teacher: Read the vocabulary words that label each pot. Then have children read the words on the potatoes and write each word on the correct pot. Have children explain why they wrote each word on the pot they did.

47

1 Which picture shows a **surplus** of food?

    ○   ○   ○

2 Which picture shows a **sliver** of cheese?

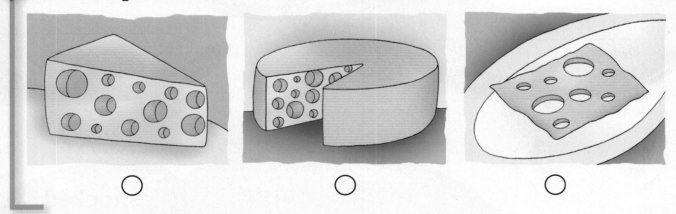

    ○   ○   ○

3 Which picture shows a **tremendous** cat?

    ○   ○   ○

Teacher: Read aloud each numbered item and have children fill in the bubble under the best picture.

4 Which picture shows a girl who is **amazed**?

◯ ◯ ◯

5 Which picture shows people **rearranging** things?

◯ ◯ ◯

6 Which picture shows a boy eating food that pleases his **palate**?

◯ ◯ ◯

1 Today is Pam's first day at a new school. Pam is **eager** to make new friends.

2 Mom is teaching Rob to swim. Rob is **petrified** of the water!

3 Ben and Jan are watching a show. They think the show is very **dull**.

Teacher: Read aloud each numbered item as children read along silently. Then have children circle the best picture for each numbered item. Ask children why they chose each picture they did.

Listen. Circle.

1. petrified   alert

2. dull   adventurous

3. rely   petrified

4. eager   dull

Teacher: Read aloud the two vocabulary words for each picture. Ask children to circle the word that best goes with each picture. Ask children how the word they chose goes with the picture.

1 Which picture shows a boy who is **petrified**?

○   ○   ○

2 Which picture shows people who are **adventurous**?

○   ○   ○

3 Which picture shows a girl having a **dull** time?

○   ○   ○

Teacher: Read aloud each numbered item and have children fill in the bubble under the best picture.

4 Which picture shows a girl **alerting** her dad?

○   ○   ○

5 Which picture shows a boy **relying** on his mom?

○   ○   ○

6 Which picture shows a boy who is **eager** to start the day?

○   ○   ○

1 Write the word that is like the word **tumble**.

smile

roll   rest

poke

_____

- - - - - - - - - - - - - - - - - -

_____

2 Write the words that are like the word **appear**.

_____

- - - - - - - - - - - - - - - - - -

_____

fly above

give to

fall down

show up

3 Write the word that is like the word **relax**.

fight

rest

work

study

_____

- - - - - - - - - - - - - - - - - -

_____

Teacher: Read aloud each numbered item. Have children read the answer choices independently and write the best answer for each item. Then have children explain their choices.

Lily Helps Mitch

Mitch finished all his work.
He could do anything he wanted.
So he hurried to the park.

Uh oh! Mitch's lunchbox broke!
"Hi!" a girl said. "My name is Lily."
Lily wanted to help Mitch.

Lily put Mitch's lunch in his hat.
Mitch can use his hat as a lunchbox!
"Thanks, Lily!" Mitch said.

1 Which word best tells about Mitch's time at the park?

tumble   leisure   outgoing

2 Which word best tells about Lily?

outgoing   relax   tumble

3 Which word best tells about Lily putting Mitch's lunch in his hat?

relax   appear   resourceful

Teacher: Have children read the story independently. Ask a volunteer to read each question aloud. Then read the word choices to children and have them circle the best answer. Ask children why they chose the words they did.

55

1 Which picture shows a dog **relaxing**?

○   ○   ○

2 Which picture shows a parade **appearing**?

○   ○   ○

3 Which picture shows a monkey **tumbling**?

○   ○   ○

Teacher: Read aloud each numbered item and have children fill in the bubble under the best picture.

4 Which picture shows a girl in her **leisure** time?

○   ○   ○

5 Which picture shows a boy being **resourceful**?

○   ○   ○

6 Which picture shows a girl who is **outgoing**?

○   ○   ○

1 Cindi and Mark found a book in the backyard. Cindi is very **observant**. Mark is not.

2 Grandpa opened the big door to his house. Once inside he knew his arm was **strained**.

3 Mom took Pat to visit Ann in the city. Ann works in a **skyscraper**.

Teacher: Read aloud each numbered item as children read along silently. Then have children circle the best picture for each numbered item. Ask children why they chose each picture they did.

1 Jeff took a **pleasant** walk with his dad.

_____

They had a _____ time.

nice

busy

fast

2 Kim **glimpsed** at the car that went by.

_____

She _____ again to see

if it was her dad.

called

laughed

looked

3 Ben thought the bike was **grand**.

_____

"What a _____ gift!"

he said.

funny

poor

great

4 Nan is very **observant**.

_____

She _____ everything

around her.

cleans

watches

colors

Teacher: Read aloud each numbered item. Then have children read the answer choices and write the best answer to complete each sentence. Have children explain why they wrote the words they did.

59

1 Which picture shows a boy being **observant**?

     ○   ○   ○

2 Which picture shows a girl **glimpsing**?

     ○   ○   ○

3 Which picture shows a boy having a **pleasant** time?

     ○   ○   ○

Teacher: Read aloud each numbered item and have children fill in the bubble under the best picture.

4 Which picture shows children **straining**?

○ ○ ○

5 Which picture shows a **skyscraper**?

○ ○ ○

6 Which picture shows the most **grand** vase of flowers?

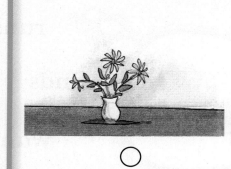  

○ ○ ○

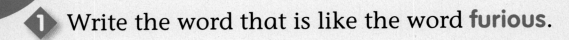

1 Write the word that is like the word **furious**.

sleepy

happy

cold

mad

_____

- - - - - - - - - - - - - - - - -

_____

2 Write the word of the one that can be **gullible**.

_____

- - - - - - - - - - - - - - - - -

_____

boy

hat

bird

paper

3 Write the word that is like the word **longs**.

runs

finds

wants

eats

_____

- - - - - - - - - - - - - - - - -

_____

Teacher: Read aloud each numbered item. Have children read the answer choices independently and write the best answer for each item. Then have children explain their choices.

62

1 It was hard for Jack to **admit** that he lost the book.

_____

But he had to _____ his mom.

thank
send
tell

2 The fox was **cunning**.

_____

He was able to _____ all the other animals.

trick
help
feed

3 Do not be **gullible**.

_____

You should not _____ that silly story.

write
believe
bring

4 Kim **realized** she didn't feel well.

_____

That night she _____ she had a bad cold.

knew
dreamed
heard

Teacher: Read aloud each numbered item. Then have children read the answer choices and write the best answer to complete each sentence. Have children explain why they wrote the words they did.

1 Which picture shows a boy being **cunning**?

○   ○   ○

2 Which picture shows a girl who **longs** for something?

○   ○   ○

3 Which picture shows a girl who just **realized** something?

○   ○   ○

Teacher: Read aloud each numbered item and have children fill in the bubble under the best picture.

4 Which picture shows a girl being **gullible**?

○   ○   ○

5 Which picture shows a woman who is **furious**?

○   ○   ○

6 Which picture shows a boy who is **admitting** something?

○   ○   ○

1

Jill gave her dog a new collar with bells.

Everyone liked the ringing bells.

Tom gave his cat a collar with bells.

Linda gave her turtle one, too.

Soon everyone's pets wore collars with bells!

"I am tired of bells," Jill said.

Jill gave her dog a new collar— with **NO** bells!

entertain

gather

fad

romp

household

creative

2

Joe and Matt live in a house with Mom and Dad.

Grandpa is coming to live with them.

Grandpa is bringing his two cats.

Will there be room for everyone?

Yes! They are happy to live all together.

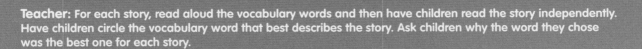

Teacher: For each story, read aloud the vocabulary words and then have children read the story independently. Have children circle the vocabulary word that best describes the story. Ask children why the word they chose was the best one for each story.

Listen. Circle.

1 creative   romp

2 fad   gather

3 gather   entertain

4 creative   romp

Teacher: Read aloud the two vocabulary words for each picture. Ask children to circle the word that best goes with each picture. Ask children how the word they chose goes with the picture.

67

Show What You Know

Listen. Fill in the bubble.

1 Which picture shows horses **romping**?

◯   ◯   ◯

2 Which picture shows a girl following a **fad**?

◯   ◯   ◯

3 Which picture shows a squirrel **gathering** something?

◯   ◯   ◯

Teacher: Read aloud each numbered item and have children fill in the bubble under the best picture.

4 Which picture shows part of a **household**?

○ ○ ○

5 Which picture shows someone **entertaining**?

○ ○ ○

6 Which picture shows somebody doing something **creative**?

○ ○ ○

Harry Is Hungry

Harry the horse lived in a field.
He had plenty of grass to eat.
But Harry was tired of eating grass.

So Harry walked to Farmer Emily's garden.
Mmmmm! Tasty flowers were everywhere!
But Harry should not eat them.

Harry looked very sad.
Farmer Emily felt sorry for Harry.
So she gave Harry some yummy
flowers to eat!

1 Which word best tells about where Harry lives?

tempting   pasture   velvet

2 Which word best tells about the flowers?

scrap   provide   tempting

3 Which word best tells what Farmer Emily did for Harry?

provide   mandatory   pasture

Teacher: Have children read the story independently. Ask a volunteer to read each question aloud. Then read the word choices to children and have them circle the best answer. Ask children why they chose the words they did.

1 It is **mandatory** that we keep quiet in line.

_____

We _____ talk.

will
cannot
must

2 Anna will **provide** our lunches today.

_____

We do not have to _____ them.

lose
forget
bring

3 My new shoes are made of **velvet**.

_____

They are very _____ and fuzzy.

soft
shiny
cold

4 Mark picked up some **scraps** of paper.

_____

These pieces were _____ over from cutting out paper stars.

left
stepped
tripped

Teacher: Read aloud each numbered item. Then have children read the answer choices and write the best answer to complete each sentence. Have children explain why they wrote the words they did.

1 Which picture shows an animal in a **pasture**?

○   ○   ○

2 Which picture shows a girl wearing **velvet**?

○   ○   ○

3 Which picture shows a blanket in **scraps**?

○   ○   ○

Teacher: Read aloud each numbered item and have children fill in the bubble under the best picture.

4 Which picture shows children doing something **mandatory**?

    ◯   ◯   ◯

5 Which picture shows something **tempting**?

    ◯   ◯   ◯

6 Which picture shows a girl **providing** something?

 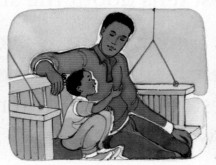 

    ◯   ◯   ◯

Flutter's Flight

Flutter is a tiny butterfly.
Her wings are light and thin.
One day, she flew over a field.

Flutter flew and flew.
The other side of the field
was very far away.
She stopped to rest on a rock.

Flutter saw a beautiful flower.
She wanted to find out about the flower.
She flew close and looked at it carefully.

1 Which word best tells about Flutter?

vast   delicate   accomplish

2 Which word best tells about the size of the field?

enhance   investigate   vast

3 Which word best tells what Flutter did when she saw the flower?

investigate   variety   delicate

Teacher: Have children read the story independently. Ask a volunteer to read each question aloud. Then read the word choices to children and have them circle the best answer. Ask children why they chose the words they did.

Listen. Circle.

1

variety   accomplish

2

investigate   vast

3

vast   enhance

4

accomplish   delicate

Teacher: Read aloud the two vocabulary words for each picture. Ask children to circle the word that best goes with each picture. Ask children how the word they chose goes with the picture.

1 Which picture shows a **variety** of balls?

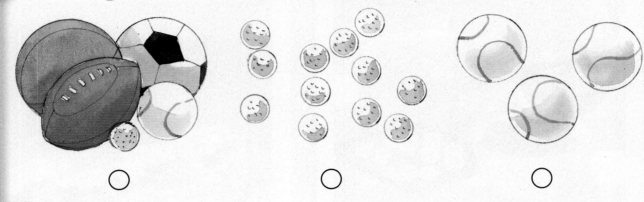

○   ○   ○

2 Which picture shows a **vast** forest?

○   ○   ○

3 Which picture shows a boy who is trying to **investigate**?

○   ○   ○

Teacher: Read aloud each numbered item and have children fill in the bubble under the best picture.

4 Which picture shows a girl playing with something that is **delicate**?

○　　　　　　　○　　　　　　　○

5 Which picture shows the house that has been **enhanced**?

○　　　　　　　○　　　　　　　○

6 Which picture shows a boy who has **accomplished** something?

○　　　　　　　○　　　　　　　○

1 A girl won a race. When she got her ribbon, she was **humble**.

2 A boy painted a picture. He showed it to his teacher. It was a good picture, so she **flattered** the boy.

3 A boat was sailing on the sea. There was a **mighty** storm.

Teacher: Read aloud each numbered item as children read along silently. Then have children circle the best picture for each numbered item. Ask children why they chose each picture they did.

Listen. Read. Write.

enormous

frighten

boast

large

scare

huge

brag

shock

giant

Teacher: Read the vocabulary words that label each shelf. Then have children read the words on the crowns and write each word on the correct shelf. Have children explain why they wrote each word on the shelf they did.

79

Show What You Know

Listen. Fill in the bubble.

1 Which picture shows a boy trying to **frighten** someone?

◯　　　◯　　　◯

2 Which picture shows an **enormous** building?

◯　　　◯　　　◯

3 Which picture shows a **mighty** wind?

◯　　　◯　　　◯

Teacher: Read aloud each numbered item and have children fill in the bubble under the best picture.

4 Which picture shows a girl **boasting**?

        ○   ○   ○

5 Which picture shows a girl being **flattered**?

        ○   ○   ○

6 Which picture shows a boy who is **humble**?

        ○   ○   ○

scamper

shrewd

run

hurry

rush

smart

clever

wise

Teacher: Read the vocabulary words that label each bookcase. Then have children read the words on the books and write each word on a shelf in the correct case. Have children explain why they wrote each word on the case they did.

1 I was **frantic** when I could not find my cat.
_____

I was _____ I would

never see her again!

afraid
glad
careful

2 Rita ate a **savory** bowl of chili.
_____

It was very _____.

cold
bad
tasty

3 Kate was **determined** to buy her

dad a jacket.
_____

She had _____

it was the perfect gift.

sung
called
decided

4 Carlos was **stunned** when his parents

gave him a new puppy.
_____

He was very _____.

slow
surprised
silly

Teacher: Read aloud each numbered item. Then have children read the answer choices and write the best answer to complete each sentence. Have children explain why they wrote the words they did.

Show What You Know

Listen. Fill in the bubble.

1 Which picture shows a man **determined** to climb a mountain?

○   ○   ○

2 Which picture shows a girl who is **stunned**?

○   ○   ○

3 Which picture shows a **savory** dish of food?

○   ○   ○

Teacher: Read aloud each numbered item and have children fill in the bubble under the best picture.

4 Which picture shows a **shrewd** man?

○ ○ ○

5 Which picture shows animals **scampering**?

○ ○ ○

6 Which picture shows a girl who is **frantic**?

○ ○ ○

1

Sue saw a beautiful bird fly past her window.

She went outside to see the bird again.

She looked and looked for the bird.

Then she spotted it in a tree.

She was so happy to see the beautiful bird!

injured

contemplate

elated

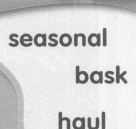

seasonal

bask

haul

2

Matt had a bag of dirty clothes in the bathroom.

Matt's mom asked him to move the bag.

Matt picked up the bag.

But it was very heavy.

He had to pull it behind him.

Teacher: For each story, read aloud the vocabulary words and then have children read the story independently. Have children circle the vocabulary word that best describes the story. Ask children why the word they chose was the best one for each story.

Listen. Circle.

1 haul   bask

2 seasonal   bask

3 contemplate   elated

4 haul   injured

Teacher: Read aloud the two vocabulary words for each picture. Ask children to circle the word that best goes with each picture. Ask children how the word they chose goes with the picture.

1 Which picture shows an **injured** boy?

○　　　　　○　　　　　○

2 Which picture shows an animal **basking**?

○　　　　　○　　　　　○

3 Which picture shows children **hauling** something?

○　　　　　○　　　　　○

Teacher: Read aloud each numbered item and have children fill in the bubble under the best picture.

4 Which of these is a **seasonal** thing to do?

○ ○ ○

5 Which picture shows a girl who is **elated**?

○ ○ ○

6 Which picture shows someone **contemplating** something?

○ ○ ○

Listen. Read. Write.

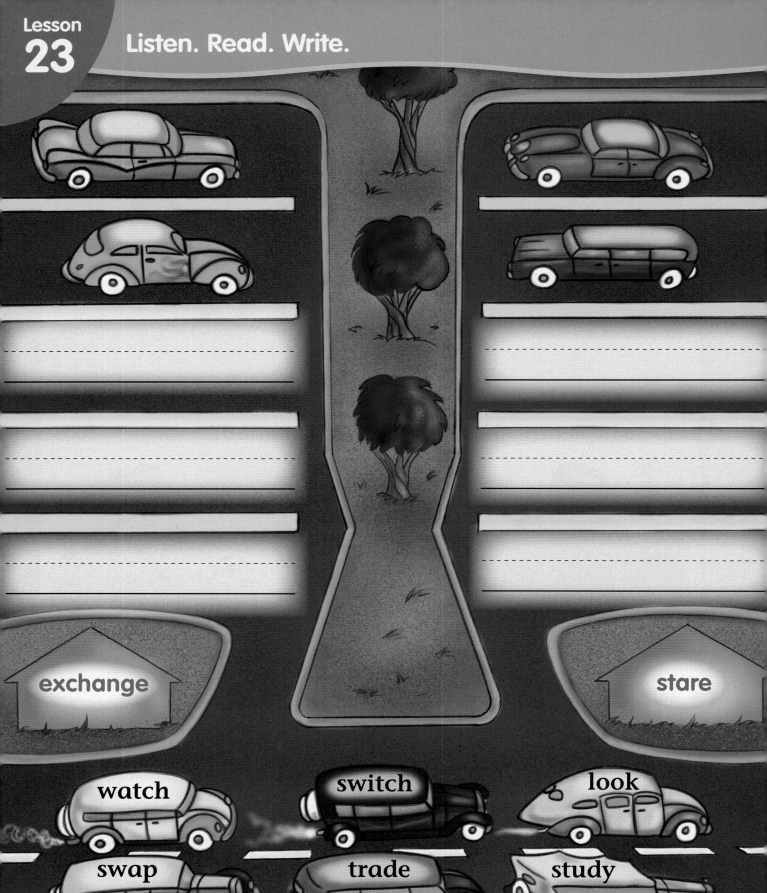

exchange

stare

watch

switch

look

swap

trade

study

Teacher: Read aloud the vocabulary words on the orange arrows that label the two parking lots. Then have children read the words on the cars and write each word in the correct parking lot. Have children explain why they wrote each word in the parking lot they did.

Listen. Read. Write.

1 After the hard race, Kim felt **relief**.
_____

She was _____ it was over.

sad

happy

mad

2 Tran **memorized** his telephone number.
He wanted to know it without having
_____

to _____ at it.

take

get

look

3 Before school, Kate felt **anxious**.
But everyone was so nice that soon
_____

Kate didn't feel _____.

lazy

surprised

worried

4 Lisa's grandma **regretted** that she
couldn't come to one of Lisa's games.
_____

Lisa's grandma felt _____.

afraid

sorry

glad

Teacher: Read aloud each numbered item. Then have children read the answer choices and write the best answer to complete each sentence. Have children explain why they wrote the words they did.

1 Which picture shows someone **staring** at the dinosaur?

○   ○   ○

2 Which picture shows someone feeling **anxious** about something?

○   ○   ○

3 Which picture shows something that the girl will likely **regret**?

○   ○   ○

Teacher: Read aloud each numbered item and have children fill in the bubble under the best picture.

4 Which people look like they need some **relief**?

○   ○   ○

5 Which picture shows someone who has **memorized** the music?

○   ○   ○

6 Which picture shows two children **exchanging** something?

○   ○   ○

Teacher: Read the vocabulary words that label each shelf. Then have children read the words in the drums and write each word on the correct shelf. Have children explain why they wrote each word on the shelf they did.

WHAT A NOISE!

Oscar was trying to sleep.
Bzzz! Bzzz! Someone was sawing.
Bang! Bang! Someone was hammering.

Daisy's friends were building a stage.
Oscar was very angry about the noise.
"Don't be upset," Daisy said. "We are
done building now."

Daisy and her friends climbed onto the stage.
They began to sing and play guitars.
"Ah ha! This beautiful music will help
me sleep!" Oscar said.

1 Which word best tells what Oscar hears at first?

commotion   harmony   soothe

2 Which word best tells what Daisy tries to do for Oscar?

fret   soothe   conflict

3 Which word best tells what Oscar heard at the end?

harmony   commotion   protest

Teacher: Have children read the story independently. Ask a volunteer to read each question aloud. Then read the
word choices to children and have them circle the best answer. Ask children why they chose the words they did.

Show What You Know

Listen. Fill in the bubble.

1 Which picture shows a group that is in **harmony**?

○　　　　　　○　　　　　　○

2 Which picture shows a boy and girl in a **conflict**?

○　　　　　　○　　　　　　○

3 Which picture shows a **commotion**?

○　　　　　　○　　　　　　○

Teacher: Read aloud each numbered item and have children fill in the bubble under the best picture.

4 Which picture shows a boy who is **fretting**?

◯　　　　◯　　　　◯

5 Which picture shows people who are **protesting**?

◯　　　　◯　　　　◯

6 Which picture shows someone who is **soothing** another person?

◯　　　　◯　　　　◯

Words I Have Learned

A

accomplish
admire
admit
adventurous
alert
amazed
amble
anxious
appear
artistic
astonished

B

bask
boast

C

capture
caution
certain
challenge
chuckle
clumsy
coincidence
comforting
commotion
complain

conflict
contemplate
convince
creative
crouch
cunning

D

deceive
delicate
delightful
deserve
destroy
determined
disguise
dissolve
disturb
dreadful
dull
dwell

E

eager
elated
enhance
enormous
entertain
exaggerate
exchange
expression

F

fad
fierce
flatter
fleet
frantic
fret
frighten
furious

G

gather
ghastly

glimmer
glimpse
gobble
grand
grateful
gullible

H

harmony
haul
household
humble

I

injured
inquire
investigate
invisible
irk

L

leisure
lively
longs

M

mandatory
memorize

mighty
mound

N

nibble

O

observant
observe
outgoing
outsmart

P

palate
pasture
patient
perform
petrified
plead
pleasant
preposterous
pride
protest
provide

Q

quiver

R

realize
rearrange
regret
relax
relief
rely
rescue
resourceful
ridiculous
romp

S

savory
scamper
scold
scrap
scrumptious
scrunched
seasonal
serenade
shelter
shrewd
skyscraper
sliver
sloppy
sly
soothe

spangled
sprinkle
squiggle
stare
strain
stunned
surplus
survive
suspend
suspense
swift

T

tempting
tidy
tremendous
tribute
tumble

V

variety
vast
velvet
versatile

W

wander

My Favorite Words

Teacher: Invite children to tell favorite words they have learned. Ask them to explain why these words are favorites—are they fun to say, are there lots of times when they can use them, or do they just make them happy? Then help children write the words on this list. Encourage children to add to their lists as they learn to use new words, both in and out of the classroom.